INDIA
the land

Bobbie Kalman

The Lands, Peoples, and Cultures Series

Crabtree Publishing Company

The Lands, Peoples, and Cultures Series
Created by Bobbie Kalman

Written by
Bobbie Kalman
Christine Arthurs
Margaret Hoogeveen

Editor-in-Chief
Bobbie Kalman

Editors
Christine Arthurs
Margaret Hoogeveen

Design
Heather Delfino

Pasteup
Adriana Longo

Printer
Worzalla Publishing Company
Stevens Point, Wisconsin

Illustrations
Halina Below-Spada: Back cover
John Mantha: p. 5

Photography acknowledgments
Cover: Tony Stone Worldwide/Masterfile
Chris Beeman: p.13(bottom); Ken Faris: p.13(top), 25(top and bottom), 7, 18;
Jeremy Ferguson/First Light: p.22; Four by Five: p.6; David Gledhill: p.4, 26;
Catriona Gordon: Title page, p.11(bottom), p.24; Ron Hayes: p.13(middle);
Susan Hughes: p.27(top); Courtesy of India Tourist Organization: p.19, 30;
Sudha and Abdullah Khandwani: p.11(top), p.30(inset); Eric Melis: p.8;
Larry Rossignol: p.10, 14, 15, 20; Royal Ontario Museum: p.23; Shostal/Four by Five: p.15;
Mike Silver: p.9, 21, 27(inset); Dave Taylor: p.28, 29; Medford Taylor/Four by Five: p.16.

Pictured on the front cover is Jaipur Palace. India's national bird, the peacock, is portrayed above the doorway. A stylized peacock is shown on the back cover, and a peacock motif appears in the heading of every section.

For the Karsons
Martha, Al, Cessa, and Miranda

Cataloguing in Publication Data

Kalman, Bobbie, 1947-
    India, the land

(Lands, peoples, and cultures series)
Includes index.

ISBN 0-86505-210-7 (bound) ISBN 0-86505-290-5 (pbk.)
1. India - Description and travel - 1981-   -
Juvenile literature. I. Title. II. Series.

DS407.K35 1990   j954

Published by
Crabtree Publishing Company

1110 Kamato Road	350 Fifth Avenue	73 Lime Walk
Unit 4	Suite 3308	Headington,
Mississauga, Ontario	New York	Oxford 0X3 7AD
Canada L4W 2P3	N.Y. 10118	United Kingdom

Contents

India is a land of great variety. Within its borders snowy mountain peaks tower over lush green valleys; fertile plains contrast with treeless deserts. Tropical rain forests add to the fascinating landscape. All this variety exists in India because it is a huge country. It is the seventh-largest country in the world and has the second-largest population.

The Ganges River flows through northern India. The land along its banks is the most crowded in the world.

India is a land of endless contrasts. The past of this ancient land seems to exist alongside its present. Its peaceful villages preserve India's heritage, whereas its huge, modern cities welcome progress. Artisans skilled in ancient crafts live side by side with professionals who use the latest technology. Swift jets fly high above camel caravans slowly making their way across the Deccan Plateau.

India is located on the southern edge of the continent of Asia. A major portion of the country is a huge peninsula. A peninsula is a piece of land that is attached to the mainland but extends into the sea. This part of India has the shape of an upside-down triangle jutting into the Indian Ocean. Off India's west coast is the Arabian Sea; off the east coast is the Bay of Bengal. India shares its borders with Pakistan, Afghanistan, China, Nepal, Bhutan, Burma, and Bangladesh. Just off India's southern tip is the small island nation of Sri Lanka.

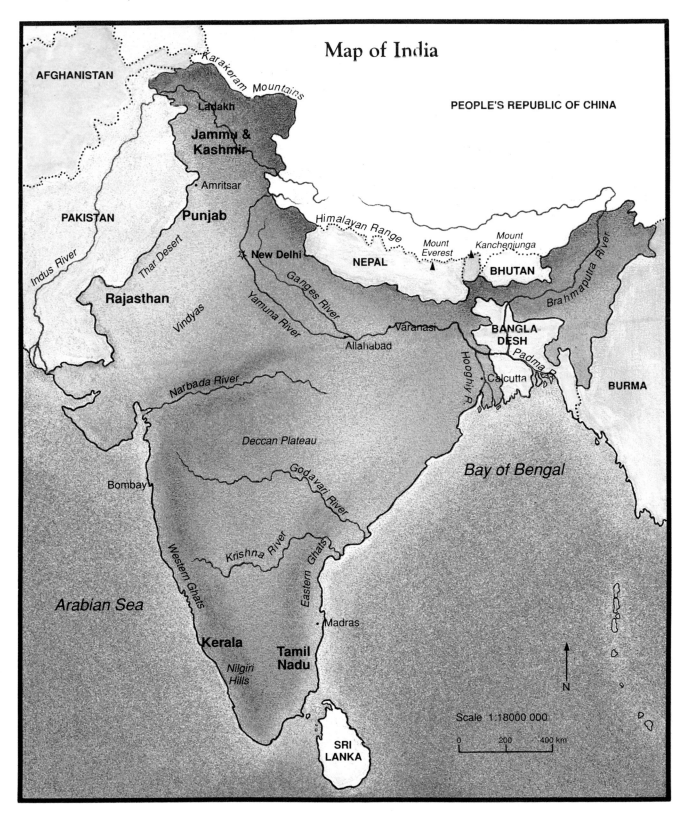

Map of India

Mountains, valleys, deserts, and tropics

Across the northern part of India are the world's highest mountains, the Himalayas. This enormous mountain range serves as a natural border between India and its neighbors. Some scientists believe that the lower part of India used to be an island. Over millions of years this island moved towards, and crashed into, Asia. The collision caused the earth to buckle where the two land masses met, forcing up a ridge of towering mountains.

The Himalayas are not only the tallest, they are also the youngest mountains in the world. They are higher and steeper than older, weather-worn mountain ranges. Because the earth continues to shift, the Himalayas still grow a few centimeters each year, although wind and rain wear them down as fast as they grow.

(above) A camel and its owner take a brief rest before traveling on. Camels are the most practical beasts of burden in the desert regions of India. (See page 31.)

In the ancient Indian Sanscrit language the word *himalaya* means "home of snow." The Great Himalayas, averaging 6100 meters (20,000 feet), are covered with snow all year round. Kanchenjunga, the tallest mountain in India, is part of the Himalayas. At 8598 meters (28,209 feet) it is only 300 meters (984 feet) shorter than Mount Everest. As you move south, the Himalayas become smaller.

A range of ranges

The Himalayas, together with several other ranges, make up one sixth of India's land area. The Karakoram Mountains are located just west of the Himalayas, and the Vindyas separate the peninsula from northern India. Along the sides of the peninsula are the Western and Eastern Ghats. *Ghat* means "step." In a country with mountains as high as the Himalayas, you can understand why smaller mountains might be called "steps."

Pale mists, bright flowers

The Nilgiri Hills are found at the southern tip of India, where the Western and Eastern Ghats meet. These rounded slopes are known as the Blue Hills because they are often covered by a veil of blue mist. Where there are mountains, there must be valleys, and India has some of the most beautiful valleys in the world. In summer the Vale of Kashmir in the foothills of the Himalayas is covered with a blanket of bright orange and yellow sunflowers.

Bone dry and baking hot

Two huge areas, the Thar Desert and the Deccan Plateau, are the hottest and driest areas of India. The Deccan Plateau, which covers most of the Indian peninsula, is barren with the exception of an occasional tuft of grass or scrub. The sun bakes the plateau, and temperatures rise as high as 45°C (113°F).

The Thar Desert is located in northwestern India. It only receives about five centimeters (two inches) of rain a year, and sometimes none at all. The temperatures can rise above a scorching 48°C (118°F). It is so hot that people carry jugs of drinking water wherever they go. These clay jugs allow moisture to seep out through their sides. When the water on the outside evaporates, it cools the water inside the jar. In the dry, hot areas of India, people must drink up to four liters (one gallon) of water every day, or they might dry out!

The heartland of India

The largest plain in the world, called the Gangetic Plain, is located directly below the Himalayas. It is sometimes called the heartland of India because it is fertile and vital to the country. For thousands of years water from melting snow has been flowing down from the Himalayas. As it travels across the land on its way to the sea, it leaves behind rich deposits. This process created a highly productive agricultural region. Three great rivers, the Brahmaputra, the Indus, and the Ganges, continue to fertilize the flat countryside of both India and its neighbors as they flow through the plains.

Lush rain forests are found on many of India's hills and along the coastlines. Every day these three boys walk home from school through the forest.

A tropical climate

Because India is located near the equator, the country has a tropical climate. Tropical climates are characterized by hot temperatures, dry winters, and wet summers. Spring is the hottest time of year. It is dry and dusty, and everyone feels tired and worn out. In June the wet season arrives. The rain comes down in buckets, and the farmers are pleased. The cool, dry winter begins in October. Nights can be chilly. Even though this general description applies to almost all of India, the climate still varies from region to region. For instance, in Kerala the jungle remains lush even in the dry winter season. At the same time of year people go skiing in the snowy mountain region in the north.

Rivers, a source of life

Water is an important source of life. It is especially precious in India because water supplies often run low. During the dry season much of the country suffers from scorching heat and lack of water. Rivers become mere trickles, plants shrivel up, and many people go hungry because crops cannot grow.

The rainy season

In June the arrival of the monsoon season brings relief. A monsoon is a wind that picks up great amounts of water as it blows across the ocean. When the heavy, purple clouds finally burst, rain comes pouring down in endless torrents, bringing the dusty earth back to life. The monsoon lasts until October.

Many areas rely entirely on the monsoon rains to provide moisture for their crops. Sometimes the monsoon enables farmers to grow a second harvest so there will be enough food to last throughout the dry season. The rains can be a mixed blessing, however. Hard-hit communities suffer from severe flooding, which causes soil erosion, damage to homes and property, traffic accidents, and drownings.

Water management

Every year India must face the challenge of the never-ending cycle of wet and dry seasons. To manage their precious water supply, Indians build dams and reservoirs to store rain water for future use. Irrigation systems channel water to farmers' fields. Rivers, reservoirs, and wells provide the water for the irrigation canals. Well water comes from ground water, which is water that is absorbed by the earth when it rains.

Misusing well water

Recently, many wells have been dug in India. Some deep wells use up valuable ground water, robbing the land of the moisture needed to keep it fertile. Plant and tree roots in the surrounding areas have difficulty reaching moisture. As a result, vegetation dies, and the land turns into desert. The misuse of well water has become a big problem. Large plantations use more than their fair share of water, so small farmers cannot get enough to grow their crops.

Pilgrims travel to the city of Varanasi to wade in the sacred river water of the Ganges River. The water here is considered to be holier than anywhere else.

Every year during the rainy season India must cope with the costly problems caused by too much water.

Mighty rivers

The Ganges, the Brahmaputra, and the Indus rivers are all fed by melting glaciers in the Himalayas. India gets its name from the Indus River because the original Indian civilization began in the Indus Valley. Today the Indus flows mainly through Pakistan, but its upper part winds through northern India. Like the Indus River, the Brahmaputra only flows through a small part of India. At 2900 kilometers (1,802 miles) it is one of the longest rivers in the world.

The Ganges River is 2506 kilometers (1,557 miles) long. It runs eastward through mountain valleys and across the fertile Gangetic Plain. The land along its banks is the most crowded area in the world. The Ganges eventually combines with the Brahmaputra and becomes the Padma River, which empties into the Bay of Bengal in Bangladesh. The Ganges and Padma rivers remain mighty even in the dry season and often burst their banks in the wet season.

From trickles to torrents

There are many other rivers in India, such as the Tapti, Narbada, Gadavari, and Krishna. These rain-fed rivers shrink in the dry season because there is not enough rain or melting snow at their sources to feed them all year round. During the rainy season they are transformed from trickles into gushing torrents. Many of India's powerful rivers have been dammed and are used to generate hydro-electric power.

Holy rivers

Water is so precious in India that rivers are considered sacred. For instance, the name Brahmaputra means "son of Brahma," the Hindu creator god. The Ganges is the most holy river of all. According to Hindu legend, the Ganges River once flowed through heaven. Many people make pilgrimages to visit holy places along this river.

India's people

India is a densely populated country. With more than eight hundred million people, it has the second-largest population in the world. Only China has more people. India is smaller than China and, therefore, more crowded. Approximately two hundred and fifty people live in each square kilometer (about half a square mile) of India. This calculation is called the average population density.

India's population has tripled in the twentieth century. If it continues to grow at this rate, it will reach one billion by the year 2000! By the middle of the twenty-first century India is expected to have the largest population in the world.

India is teeming with people. As the day begins, this rush-hour crowd spills out of a train station.

Ancient ancestors

The people of India do not all share the same background. The majority of Indians can trace their ancestry back thousands of years. The first inhabitants of India were nomadic tribes known as Adivasis. Today the Adivasis live in small self-contained communities scattered throughout the country. There are about four hundred groups left, making up about seven percent of the total population. Their languages and customs are different from those of other Indians.

A people called the Dravidians lived as a well-developed society in the Indus Valley about 4500 years ago. About a thousand years later a lighter-skinned nomadic tribe from central Asia, known as the Aryans, invaded the

Dravidian settlements. The Dravidians moved south, and the Aryans settled throughout the rest of India. Hundreds of years later Muslim invaders arrived, taking control of northern India. Over many centuries the cultures of these groups blended together in many ways.

The many faces of India

The long and complicated history of the Indian people resulted in the rich and varied culture of present-day India. Although Hindi is considered the main language, fourteen other official languages and countless dialects are spoken throughout the country. People have different customs, practice a number of religions, and celebrate a variety of festivals.

Despite all these differences, Indians are held together by many common threads. More than three quarters of the population follow the Hindu religion. Only eleven percent of the population is Muslim, but the Muslim influence is very strong. India's people also share a common history and similar goals for the future of their country.

(right) This girl wears the traditional clothing of her region.

(below) These Ladakhi children say hello in the Indian way.

 # A country of villages

Across the vast expanse of India there are more than half a million small villages. Most of them have fewer than one thousand inhabitants each, yet in total, more than three quarters of the country's population live in these rural settlements. Every one, from tiny hamlet to large town, is a unique community. Some are coastal fishing villages; others are farming towns.

Community living

An Indian village is a close-knit community. The homes are usually clustered together around a village square. From here the farmers walk to their fields every day and the fishermen head out to catch fish in nearby waters. Most village families have lived in the same village for countless generations. Each generation passes on the family's skills, knowledge, and land to its children. Most villagers live off the land, but in larger villages artisans such as weavers, potters, shopkeepers, and smiths provide services necessary for the well-being of the community. Farmers sell their produce, and vendors sell their wares at busy open-air markets called bazaars.

Changing village lifestyle

For centuries, time seemed to stand still in the rural villages. Each community took care of its own needs and rarely had contact with outsiders. Although much has stayed the same, villagers are now experiencing many changes.

Today residents can travel quite easily from village to village using buses, bicycles, and scooters. Many villages have some electricity, a few phones, and a government-supplied television for the community.

New covered wells

In the past, people had to carry water from faraway rivers or depend on open wells in the community. Open wells were a source of disease because bacteria thrived in them. To prevent disease, the government started a program to provide every village with a covered well. A covered well consists of a very long tube sunk deep in the ground through which water can be pumped. In the past twenty years thousands and thousands of these wells have been installed. Today ninety percent of India's villages have covered wells powered by electric or hand-operated pumps.

A long way to go

Although some aspects of village life are improving, communities still face serious problems. Sewage- and garbage-disposal systems do not exist in most villages. This is not only unhealthy, it is also harmful to the environment. Both the land and water surrounding the villages are becoming contaminated with the waste produced by a growing population.

(opposite) Villagers go to the market or bazaar to buy food, conduct business, and catch up on the latest news.

12

Growing cities

Bursting at the seams

Some of India's cities have been around for hundreds of years; others are relatively new. In older cities palaces, temples, and ancient city walls still stand as reminders of India's past. In the new sections modern buildings create a different skyline. Whether old or new, all of India's cities share a common characteristic—they are growing at an incredibly fast rate. As a result, Indian cities have become overcrowded, and millions of people have nowhere to live.

India's capital

The capital city of India is New Delhi. It is located on the banks of the Yamuna River, a tributary of the Ganges. New Delhi has only been the capital of India since 1931. It is made up of two cities—a modern city that is less than a hundred years old and a walled city, sometimes called Old Delhi, that has existed for centuries.

The legacy of Shah Jahan

At one time Old Delhi was the home of the Mogul emperors. At that time it was known as Shahjahanabad because it was named after Shah Jahan, the ruler who had this walled city built. At its core was a magnificent palace constructed from red sandstone and aptly named the Red Fort. Emperors ruled from the fabulous Peacock Throne, studded with sapphires, rubies, emeralds, and pearls. The Red Fort now houses museums and shops.

(opposite) Bombay's natural harbor has made it the nation's trading capital.

The gateway to India

Bombay, a city on the Arabian Sea, was built on the islands surrounding a huge natural harbor. In the past, traders came in sailing ships from distant lands. They nicknamed Bombay "The Gateway to India." All trading vessels anchored in the harbor before moving on to other ports to find India's spices and teas. Bombay now handles half of India's foreign trade and is still the country's main point of contact with other nations. With over ten million people, Bombay has the largest population of any Indian city.

Calcutta

The city of Calcutta is located on the Hooghly River, which empties into the Bay of Bengal. Named after the Hindu goddess Kali, Calcutta was the capital city when India was a British colony. British-styled monuments and buildings are a common sight in the older section of the city. Today Calcutta is a major center of business and culture. It is the tenth-largest urban center in the world and the only Indian city with an underground subway.

Sacred city on the Ganges

Perhaps the city that best captures the spirit of India is Varanasi. Varanasi, which is located on the Ganges River, is both ancient and holy. Hindu pilgrims from all over India travel there to worship in temples and bathe in the sacred river. Varanasi may be the oldest living city on earth.

(below) New Delhi, the capital of India, has wide, modern streets. Connaught Circus runs around the heart of the city.

From the land and sea

Three quarters of India's people make their living from the land. With a rapidly growing population, the country's farmers must work very hard to feed all the citizens. This can be a challenging task because many parts of India are too dry to support crops.

The most fertile farming areas are the Gangetic Plain, the eastern river delta by the Bay of Bengal, the Punjab, and the coastlines. Crops vary from region to region. Rice is India's primary crop; only China grows more rice than India does. About one quarter of all cultivated land is reserved for this grain. Most of India's rice is grown in the southern coastal areas and in the river delta. In drier areas, on the Deccan Plateau and in the Punjab region, wheat is the most important crop. Lentils are the other main staple of the Indian diet. They provide necessary nutrients and proteins. In the lush tropical regions all sorts of fruits and spices are grown, such as lemons, limes, jackfruit, coconuts, mangoes, bananas, sugar cane, pepper, and ginger.

Modern machines

Until recently all farming chores were done by hand with the help of water buffalo or oxen. Today tractors, threshing machines, and other types of modern equipment ease the workload on large farms. Most family farms, however, still use traditional tools and methods of farming. Many small farmers cannot afford modern equipment or the tools and parts required to fix machines when they break down. They also lack the special skills needed to operate and repair the machines. Changing from traditional methods of farming to new techniques takes a great deal of money, time, and training.

Farming problems

Indian farmers must cope with many serious problems. Their crops depend on an unpredictable supply of water. If there is a flood or a drought, crops fail. Dry regions must rely on wells, reservoirs, and irrigation systems for their water supply. Modern wells are powered by electricity, which is often in short supply.

A shortage of land

On average, farmers are not able to make an adequate living because of a grave shortage of land. After generations of dividing up the land among children, many farmers are left with tiny farms. As a result, small farmers are being forced to sell their farmland to large landowners. Others rent land from landowners who take between one third and one half of the harvest for themselves and leave very little for the farmers. This practice is called sharecropping. One of the major causes of poverty in India is that farmland is not distributed fairly. Consequently, thousands of landless farmers move to the cities each year in search of work.

(opposite) This woman spends her days bent over a rice field. Without the aid of modern farming equipment, rice farming is a back-breaking occupation.

Fishing

The seas surrounding India are valuable natural resources. Coastal fishing has recently become a profitable industry. The introduction of deep-sea fishing has greatly helped the fishing industry. Mackerel, sardines, shark, perch, and tuna are caught in the sea. Part of the catch is transported in refrigerated train compartments to markets across the country. The rest is frozen and exported to other countries. Fishermen also catch carp and catfish from inland rivers. Shrimp is the most popular seafood export. Frog legs, lobster tails, and shark fins are other Indian delicacies enjoyed by people around the world.

(below) At the end of the day giant fishing nets are hung out to dry over the sparkling sea.

One of India's greatest challenges is to provide adequate food for its ever-growing population. Forty years ago India had to buy large amounts of food from other countries because its own farms could not produce enough to feed the entire population.

The green revolution

In the 1960s India experienced the "green revolution." The green revolution is the term used to describe an enormous increase in farming production. New wells and irrigation projects, modern farming machinery, chemical fertilizers, and pesticides all made this agricultural growth possible. Scientists from Japan and Mexico developed a new type of hardy wheat grain that could produce four times the amount that ordinary wheat could produce. Indian farmers began to plant this new grain and, in less than ten years, the amount of wheat they grew doubled. The green revolution has helped make India self-sufficient in food production.

Cash instead of food?

Farmers who grow cash crops have benefited enormously from the green revolution. Cash crops are harvested in large quantities on huge plantations and then exported to other countries. Sugar cane, grown in the central regions of India, is a cash crop. It is refined and sold as packaged sugar. Tea is another example. India is famous around the world for its flavorful teas. Other cash crops include rubber, tobacco, cotton, and coffee. Although cash crops may be profitable for some, they take up land that could otherwise grow the grains, fruits, and vegetables necessary to provide a hungry nation with a balanced diet.

Some cash-crop farmers are using up too much ground water, so the land is in danger of becoming a desert. Other plantations abuse the land while trying to produce as much as possible as quickly as possible. They plant one crop right after harvesting another crop, so the soil is unable to replace its nutrients.

(opposite) It's harvest time! In the past twenty-five years India has been producing more abundant crops than ever before.

(above) Tea is a cash crop. Pickers such as this woman work on tea plantations in the Nilgiri Hills and the hilly areas of northeast India.

 # Industry

India is considered one of the top ten industrialized nations of the world. Indian companies make everything from computers to soda pop. Many industries are owned by the government, but more and more privately owned companies are being established in India.

Natural resources

One of the reasons that India has so much industry is that the country is rich in a variety of natural resources such as coal, oil, iron, and lumber. Most of India's manufacturing is based on these natural resources. Coal and oil industries provide energy for homes as well as factories. Many Indian trains and factories burn coal as fuel to operate their engines or machines. The Steel Authority of India produces steel from iron, which is used to build machines, cars, tools, and other products.

(above) Handpainted posters advertise the latest hit movies.

India exports a large portion of its raw materials to other industrialized nations, which use the raw materials to make manufactured goods. Rubber, for example, is plentiful in India. It comes from a special tree and is used to make tires, rubber boots, and all kinds of other useful products. Logging is another industry that uses natural resources. Trees are cut down, and the lumber is used to make furniture and houses in India and abroad.

Towards self-sufficiency

When India first became an independent nation, it had to import most of its manufactured goods. Today India makes its own bicycles, tractors, railway cars, scooters, and ships. It also manufactures electronics, plastics, chemicals, computers, and computer software. To build up industry, the government now encourages "joint ventures." Joint ventures

are businesses that are owned by both Indian and foreign investors. An example of a joint venture in India is the Maruti car company, which is owned by Japanese people and Indians.

The ancient textile industry

Centuries ago Indians developed weaving skills and styles that have become world famous. Cloth was woven on hand looms by a special group of artisans. Dyeing was done by another. The skills of weaving and dyeing were passed on from generation to generation.

Today the textile industry is the backbone of Indian manufacturing. India has become the second-largest cotton producer in the world. It also produces great quantities of silk and jute. Most materials are woven on machines in huge factories. Cotton fabric and other textiles are made into shirts, trousers, and dresses, which are then exported, or the material itself is shipped to clothing factories in other countries.

(above) Indian textile making has developed into an art.

Movies galore

India's film-making industry is the largest in the world and employs about three million people. Bombay is sometimes called the Hollywood of India because it releases over eight hundred films a year and distributes them worldwide. Most Indian movies are musical romances with lots of singing and dancing. Recently the film industry has expanded to include serious films that cover social conditions and problems.

Pollution

Due to the huge amount of industry in India, pollution has become a major problem. Coal-burning factories spew out dangerous fumes, covering the cities with blankets of smog. Few pollution controls exist to cope with the wastes. Toxic waste is frequently dumped into the air and water and onto the land, with little concern for the environment. Many cities still do not have adequate waste-disposal systems to cope with their garbage and sewage.

Cottage industries

India has a tradition of producing beautiful and useful products in its village cottage industries. Cottage industries are businesses that are conducted in people's homes. Most of these industries are based on ancient skills and techniques passed down through the generations. Spinning, weaving, and the creation of carpets, toys, wickerware, and pottery are just some examples of cottage industries. Today many cottage-industry products are sold in Indian cities and to other countries.

Handmade beauty

Mahatma Gandhi was a beloved national leader who led India's struggle for independence. He strongly urged Indians to maintain their traditional village crafts. He believed that developing these crafts would help villages become self-sufficient and make India strong. Today the government continues to encourage cottage industries because they provide jobs for villagers. Some village artisans are going out of business because there is not enough demand for their goods. Their wares cost more money than inexpensive, factory-made goods do. The handmade products of skilled artisans, however, are still prized for their quality and unmatched beauty. For example, handloomed *saris* are treasured by those who can afford to buy them.

Instead of having a door and windows, this shoemaker's shop is completely open to the street.

Markets, called bazaars, are part of every Indian city and large village. Bazaars are busy streets and lanes where items are bought and sold. Each street is lined with many tiny cubbyhole-like shops. Merchants also sell their goods from stalls, carts, and mats spread out on the ground.

Every imaginable kind of item can be found at an Indian bazaar. Fresh vegetables, lime juice, glittering gold and silver jewelry, garlands of marigolds, sticky sweets, clothes, and books are all for sale. Street stalls also offer a variety of services. You can get your hair cut, a letter typed, your fortune told, a tooth filled, or have a bite to eat.

Who's the better barterer?

If you shop at an Indian bazaar, you must know how to barter. When you ask the price of an item, the vendor tells you how much he or she wants for it. The cost, however, is not fixed. You are expected to say how much you are willing to pay. After some discussion, you and the vendor agree on a price, and a deal is made.

Walking through a bazaar is like being at a circus sideshow. Street performers such as acrobats and snake charmers please the crowds with their amazing feats.

Looking at a busy city street in India for the first time, you might wonder how people manage to reach their destinations. Cars, trucks, buses, bicycles, scooters, taxis, and pedestrians all compete for road space. You might see three people on a motorcycle bolting into traffic or a bicycle rickshaw squeezing its way between two moving trucks. The confusing flow of vehicles can become more congested due to wandering cows and slow-moving bullock carts. In some areas it is not unusual to find camels, mules, and elephants on the streets.

Indians often decorate their traveling machines. Regular taxicabs are yellow and black, but their interiors are adorned with pictures from magazines, dangling religious items, or sparkling trim. Trucks and carts are painted in bright reds, yellows, and blues.

Air India

By far the safest way to travel in India is by air. The national airline, Air India, flies passengers, mail, and cargo throughout India and all over the world. Altogether, India has more than eighty airports. The four largest cities have international airports.

Rural travel

With three quarters of the population living in rural villages, walking from place to place is still the main means of transportation. Riding in a bullock cart is also a common way of traveling. Bullocks are docile bulls. They can pull heavy loads and manage difficult roads. Drivers twist the animals' tails to make them go faster. Some bullock carts have wooden wheels, causing the passengers to have bumpy rides. Rubber tires make the ride more comfortable, but they are an expensive luxury that only the better-off villagers can afford. Farmers who have tractors use them for more than just plowing fields. They drive them on the roads, using them to transport both people and goods. To shield passengers from the hot sun, tractors are often equipped with umbrellas.

A far-reaching network

Since the first train tracks were laid in the 1860s, the Indian railroad has expanded enormously. Altogether there are 61 850 kilometers (38,433 miles) of track crisscrossing the country, making it the fourth-longest rail network in the world. Today Indian trains carry ten million passengers each day! Those who can afford the fare ride first class in compartments with soft, cushioned chairs. Most people, however, travel second class. Second-class cars are cheaper, but they are always crowded. Seats are not only placed side by side, but also one on top of another in bunkbed style. Some passengers stand near the wide-open doors to breathe the fresh air and avoid the cramped quarters. People who cannot afford tickets and paying passengers who cannot find seats ride on the roof. This is an extremely dangerous way to travel.

All sorts of vehicles are used in India. This camel cart can carry heavy loads.

Brimful buses

People prefer to use trains, but many also take buses. Buses are always jam-packed and stifling hot inside. They are frequently so crowded that they overflow with passengers. Besides being used for traveling between villages, buses also provide public transportation in cities. In some areas city buses resemble transport trucks with cabs at the front. Not all buses are uncomfortable, however. Many tour buses are shiny, air-conditioned coaches that show video movies during the ride.

Rocky roads

In the past, Indian villages were almost impossible to reach because there were no roads. Today most places are connected by roads, but there are still no major highways. Many country roads, full of potholes and rocks, are better suited for bullock carts than modern vehicles. Roads and bridges are often washed out during the monsoon season. City streets are paved, but traffic is so congested that at times the roads are transformed into parking lots!

(above) Traveling by bus is so popular that it is not unusual for passengers to ride on the roof.

(top) Many boats cruise the rivers of India. Large boats carry supplies of coal and timber, whereas smaller ones ferry people and their animals.

India has the highest number of traffic mishaps in the world. Poor road and rail conditions, careless driving, and vehicles that are in need of repair are the causes of many accidents. Since buses and trains are often overcrowded, the number of deaths is unusually high when accidents occur.

Examining development

India is often referred to as a "less-developed" nation. What does this mean? We use the word "develop" in many ways. For instance, photographers develop film, and organizers develop plans. Our bodies develop as we grow, and we develop as human beings through education and experiences. No matter which way we use the word "develop," it always means that a change is taking place. When we talk about the development of countries, we are referring to how nations grow and change. Every nation is growing and changing, but some countries are considered less developed than others.

What is a less-developed country?

A less-developed country is one that is unable to satisfy the basic human needs of its people such as food, shelter, proper clothing, health care, and education. As a result, less-developed countries share similar living conditions. The majority of the population earn their living by working on farms, and the cities are filled with people who cannot find work. There are not enough doctors to look after the medical needs of the people, and many citizens do not have access to clean drinking water. People live shorter lives, and many babies die each year.

It is difficult for people in less-developed countries such as India to get ahead. Many Indians spend most of their time just trying to survive. Not only must they struggle to get their daily food and water and acquire clothing and shelter, they must also try to stay healthy. People must be healthy and feel secure before they can improve their lives.

The problem of poverty

The gravest problem in less-developed countries is poverty. More than one third of the people of India live in utter poverty. Some countries are poor because they have few resources or suffer from regular physical disasters. Other countries have unstable or corrupt governments that mismanage their funds. War can be another strain that creates poor living conditions. Less-developed countries suffer from any combination of these crippling circumstances.

The legacy of colonialism

Many less-developed countries were, at one time, taken over and made colonies of more powerful countries. Their natural resources were shipped back for use in the "mother country." When they became independent nations, these ex-colonies were not nearly as well off and developed as their "mother countries." India is an example of a nation with a colonial past. Britain took India's natural resources and then sold them back to the Indians in the form of manufactured goods. For this reason, India became dependent on Britain, and its own industry was not developed.

What makes India different?

Unlike other less-developed countries, India has developed its industry to a great extent over the last forty years. Yet India is still considered a less-developed nation. Industry alone does not solve a country's problems. Most Indians remain poor even though their country produces everything from cars to computers. The kind of development that India lacks is social development. It needs to set up programs to help meet the basic needs of its people so they can improve their living conditions.

Attitudes matter

When studying poverty or development, people often make value judgments about others without realizing it. Some believe that people in less-developed nations want to copy the lifestyle of people in more-developed nations. In fact, the people who live in less-developed nations lead meaningful lives. For instance, Indians have a well-developed, ancient culture that brings them happiness and fulfillment.

Dignified aid

Development does not mean changing the values of a group of people. When people from outside a country try to help those in less-developed countries, they sometimes make the mistake of trying to change the native culture. It is important for outsiders to respect the dignity of the people to whom they are giving aid, or they can do more harm than good. Less-developed countries must find solutions that are suitable to their values and way of life.

Developing your own ideas

In your classroom or library hold a forum on poverty and development. List the advantages you and your friends have that a child your age who lives in India does not have. How might your families differ? What disadvantages might the other child be struggling against? How will these affect the rest of his or her life?

Make a list of less-developed countries. What are your reasons for putting these countries on your list? Have you made some value judgments when you gave these reasons? Make a list of your most important values and ask your neighbor to do the same. How do your values differ from his or hers? How might the values of people in one country differ from those of another country?

What changes would you like to see in your country and in the world? Why is it important for more-developed countries to aid less-developed countries? How can individuals help? After you have discussed development with your classmates, make some suggestions about how to make the world a better-developed planet.

(above) Most of India still relies on manual labor and outdated ways of doing things. A lack of modern technology can be a great disadvantage for a struggling country.

(above) Every culture has its own values. What values come through in this picture? Are they different from values in your culture?

(below) Shelter is one of the basic needs of all people. Like many others in India, this homeless family endures terrible living conditions.

 # Exotic wildlife

Some of the most exotic animals in the world come from India. At one time they were abundant in their natural habitats all over the country. The Asian lion and the Indian gazelle roamed the grasslands, whereas the camel toured the desert. Forests were alive with the roar of the elephant and the chatter of the monkey. In the jungles the wild buffalo and the mammoth one-horned rhinoceros were once found. The snow leopard made its home in the Himalayas. The panther, the cheetah, and the Royal Bengal tiger have lived in India for seventy million years. Magnificently colored exotic birds such as the peacock also added to the country's wildlife. The animal world has greatly enriched the land of India.

Where have all the animals gone?

Just as animal species all over the world are disappearing, Indian wildlife is also dwindling rapidly. Over the centuries, as the population of India increased, more and more land was cleared and settled, leaving less and less room for animal habitats. Today most of the animal habitats have disappeared to make way for farms, cities, and massive projects such as hydro-electric dams.

Overhunting is another major cause of the devastation. India has a long tradition of hunting for sport. In the past, hunting expeditions took place on the estates of the Maharajahs, or Indian princes. Europeans flocked to India in pursuit of big game.

Game reserves protect wildlife such as this Asian lion.

The royal Bengal tiger is India's national animal. Most tigers are orange and black, but this is a rare white Bengal tiger.

Protecting endangered species

Many of India's animals are now listed as endangered species. Fewer than two hundred Asian lions are left. The one-horned rhinoceros is also an endangered species, as are the black panther and leopard. To protect these and other animals, the Indian government has set up more than one hundred wildlife sanctuaries, parks, and reserves. Many of the old hunting grounds have been turned into scenic national parks. Today there are strict hunting rules. Only a certain kind and number of animals can be killed every year on special animal reserves, and hunting endangered animals is totally illegal.

Preying poachers

Despite all these protective measures poachers, people who kill wild animals illegally, make huge amounts of money. Some people are willing to pay extremely high prices for luxurious fur coats and ivory carvings.

The majestic tiger

The royal Bengal tiger is the national animal of India. This magnificent tiger is the largest member of the cat family and possesses striking stripes. Indian folklore is full of stories about the majestic ways of tigers. Yet people's high regard for the tiger has not protected it from being overhunted. In the 1970s fewer than two thousand of these animals remained in India. As a result, hunting the tiger became illegal, and tiger habitats were preserved. Thanks to Project Tiger, this majestic cat has made a remarkable comeback!

Elephants and camels

Elephants that are native to India are smaller than African elephants. For centuries Asian elephants have been trained to perform many useful tasks because they are strong and intelligent beasts. At one time they were ridden into battle by the Indian army. Today they are used in the logging industry to pull trees and haul heavy logs.

Elephant training school

Elephants begin training when they are five years old. Their trainers are called *mahouts*. At the beginning of training, a team of *mahouts* strokes the elephant over and over again until the animal gets used to the presence of people. It is bathed and scrubbed down every day as a reward for its hard work. By the end of the seven-year training period, an elephant can respond to up to forty vocal commands. A *mahout* and his sensitive student often become lifelong companions.

Long-distance loads

Camels carry people and packages across the Thar Desert. Camel caravans wind their way through dry terrain and rocky hills, loaded down with goods and dressed in elaborate garb. Like a horse, a camel wears a saddle, reins, and stirrups. The bridle is clipped onto a camel's nostrils instead of being held in its mouth because the animal is constantly chewing its cud. A proud owner also drapes a fancy saddle blanket over the camel's back. The best decorations of all are the bells that tinkle softly in the desert wind.

Camel secrets

People have often wondered how camels can travel such long distances without taking a drink. They used to think that camels stored water inside their humps. Camels do not store water; they conserve it. The fat deposits in their humps are used as energy. Camels also have flexible body temperatures and sweat very little. When they do get a chance to drink, they can slurp up a hundred liters (twenty-six gallons) of water in less than ten minutes!

One, two, three, up!

A camel gets up in three stages. First, it rises halfway up on its hind legs, causing its body to tip forward. A rider must hold on as he or she lurches forward. A beginner may be thrown over the camel's head. The animal then straightens its front legs, one at a time. After a couple of quick side-to-side motions and a sharp tip backwards, the camel has all four legs straight and is ready to go.

A ship in the desert?

A camel ride is quite a bumpy experience, but this has nothing to do with its humps. Camels walk by moving both feet on one side forward at the same time. This causes passengers to be tossed from side to side and back to front. You can understand why the camel has been called the "ship of the desert." The slower the animal walks, the bumpier the ride becomes. An experienced camel rider who knows how to move with the animal's motion will tell you that riding on a galloping camel is as "smooth as flying in a jet plane."

Camel capers

Camels are well known for their stubborn nature and nasty personalities. When they get upset, they spit, hiss, and bite. Although it is often difficult to get a camel to follow orders, cooperative ones can move quickly. The fastest camels have been clocked at speeds of over sixty-five kilometers (forty miles) per hour.

(opposite, inset) To cope with sandstorms, camels have two rows of eyelashes and are able to close their nostrils. This camel's owner has shaved the neck of his favorite animal to create a raised design.

(opposite) Elephants are often painted and decorated before they go in parades. Painted or not, elephants are always the center of attention.

Glossary

ancestry - The family line from which a person is descended

artisan - A skilled craftsperson

barter - To trade one thing for another instead of using money

civilization - A society with a well-established culture that has existed for a long period of time

contaminated - Poisoned or polluted

cottage industry - A business that is conducted in a person's home

culture - The customs, beliefs, and arts of a distinct group of people

delta - A mass of sand, mud, and soil that settles at the mouth of a river

deposit - A mass of material that builds up by a natural process

drought - An extended period when there is no rain

endangered - Very close to becoming extinct, or no longer existing as a species

erosion - The gradual washing away of soil and rocks by rain, wind, or running water

evaporate - To change from a liquid into a gas

fertilizer - Nutrients that are added to soil to make it better for growing plants

fume - A poisonous gas given off in vaporous form

generation - People born at about the same time. Grandparents, parents, and children make up three generations.

glacier - Snow that is compressed into huge rivers of ice, found in mountains and polar regions

Hinduism - An ancient Indian religion based on the holy books called the *Vedas*

industrialized - A term used to describe a society that produces manufactured goods in factories

Mogul - A Muslim empire that existed in India between the 16th and 19th centuries

monsoon - A rain-filled wind that blows inland from the ocean

Muslim - A follower of the Islamic religion

natural resource - Anything that exists in nature and is useful to human beings. Forests, mineral deposits, and water are all natural resources.

nutrient - A substance that living things need in order to grow

pesticide - A chemical that is used to kill insects to prevent them from eating plants

pilgrimage - A journey to a sacred place or shrine

plantation - A huge farm that grows cash crops and employs many workers

pollution - Waste, such as chemicals and garbage, that harms ecosystems

raw material - A substance from the earth that is not yet processed or refined

reservoir - A large, natural or human-made store of water

sanctuary - A place where wildlife can live safely

sari - The traditional garment worn by many Indian women consisting of a long cloth wrapped around the waist and draped over one shoulder

sharecropping - A type of farming whereby a portion of the harvest is given to a landowner as rent

species - A distinct animal or plant group that shares similar characteristics and can produce offspring

toxic - Poisonous

tributary - A river that flows into a larger river

tropical - Describing a hot, humid climate

urban - Relating to the city

Index

2 3 4 5 6 7 8 9 WP Printed in U.S.A. 9 8 7 6 5 4 3 2 1